Stop Guessing About Retirement

A Practical Guide to Knowing If Your Retirement Plan Really Works

RetireWise AI

Copyright

Stop Guessing About Retirement

Published by RetireWise AI

ISBN: 979-8-9969824-0-0

First Edition

A Note Before You Begin

This book is educational in nature and should not be considered individualized financial, tax, investment, or legal advice. The strategies, examples, and stories in this book are for illustrative purposes only and do not guarantee any specific outcome.

Every person's financial situation is different, and decisions about retirement should be made in consultation with a qualified financial, tax, or legal professional who understands your specific circumstances.

Neither the author nor RetireWise AI is acting as your financial advisor, and nothing in this book should be construed as a recommendation to buy, sell, or hold any investment or insurance product.

The people portrayed in this book — including Robert, Linda, Carol, James, Denise, Frank, Margaret, Tom, Susan, and Bill — are fictional composites created for illustrative purposes. They do not represent real individuals, and any resemblance to actual people is coincidental.

Dedication

To my wife —

for the years you stayed steady when I wasn't,

for believing in this book before it was one,

and for building the life I never worry about coming home to.

This one's for you.

Table of Contents

Page numbers reflect this edition's layout and may shift slightly if the document is edited.

Introduction: Why I Wrote This Book

I've lost count of how many times I've heard some version of the same sentence.

"I've worked my whole life. I've saved what I could. Am I going to be okay?"

I've heard it from people with $300,000 saved, and from people with $3 million saved. I've heard it from people who retired at 55 and people who are still working at 68 because they're afraid to stop. I've heard it in person, in emails, in comments under videos, and in the quiet pause right before someone hangs up the phone after a consultation, like they're working up the nerve to say what they really came to ask.

It's never really a question about math. It's a question about whether they can finally stop worrying.

I started RetireWise AI because I kept watching smart, careful, hardworking people torture themselves over a number nobody had ever properly explained to them. They'd read an article that said they needed a million dollars. Then a different article said two million. Then a podcast host said it depends. All of that noise, and not one clear answer to the only question that actually mattered to them.

So we built tools to help people see their own numbers clearly — real income, real expenses, real risks, tested against real life instead of a rule of thumb. And the more people we helped, the more I noticed something. The relief people felt wasn't really about the spreadsheet. It was about finally understanding their own situation well enough to trust it.

That's the whole idea behind this book.

I didn't want to write another book that tells you how to get rich, or how to pick investments, or how to beat the market. There are plenty of those already, and most of them are aimed at people with twenty or thirty years left to compound their savings, not people staring down retirement in the next five or ten.

I wanted to write the book I wish someone had handed my own clients years before they ever sat down across from me — something that walks through the actual questions people lie awake asking, in plain language, without pretending there's a magic number that makes the fear disappear.

You're going to meet several people in these pages. Robert, who hit his number and still couldn't sleep. Linda, who trusted a calculator right up until her sister asked one question it never answered. Denise and Frank, who saved the exact same amount and ended up in completely different places. None of them are real people, exactly — they're composites, built from patterns I've seen over and over in this work. But I'd bet at least one of them is going to feel uncomfortably familiar.

That's on purpose. If you see yourself in Robert's fear, or Linda's relief, or Frank's mortgage, I hope it helps to know you're not the only one who's felt that way. Almost everyone has.

My hope for this book is simple. I don't want you to close it with a bigger number in your head. I want you to close it with a clearer understanding of your own plan — what it can handle, what it can't yet, and what to do about the gap.

Retirement isn't a math problem. It's a life you're trying to protect. This book is my attempt to help you protect it with clarity instead of guesswork.

Let's start with Robert.

Chapter 1: The Million-Dollar Myth

Meet Robert

Robert is 65. He just retired after thirty-eight years at the same company. And last month, something happened that he'd been waiting for since he was in his thirties.

His accounts crossed $1,000,000.

His wife smiled and said, "You did it."

For a few hours, he believed her.

And that night, lying in bed, staring at the ceiling, Robert felt something he didn't expect.

Not relief.

Fear.

"Is this actually enough?" he thought. "What if I'm wrong? What if the market crashes next year? What if I live to ninety-five? What if I become a burden to my family?"

It was the number magazines promised.

The number coworkers admired.

The number television experts celebrated.

The number that was supposed to make the worrying stop.

And it didn't feel like the finish line he thought it would be.

It felt like the beginning of a retirement filled with questions instead of certainty.

If you've ever felt this way — like you're chasing a number, and even hitting it doesn't bring the peace you expected — you're not alone. And you're not wrong to feel that way.

Because here's the truth.

Robert wasn't asking the wrong question.

He'd been taught the wrong question.

What People Believe

Somewhere along the way, retirement got reduced to a single question:

"How much do I need to save?"

And a single answer:

"$1,000,000."

Or maybe it's $1.5 million. Or $2 million, depending on which article you read last. But it's always a number. A big, round, scary number that sits in your head like a test you haven't studied for.

The myth goes like this: hit the number, and you're safe. Miss the number, and you're in trouble.

It's simple. It's tidy. It fits in a headline.

It's comforting because it's simple.

Real retirement rarely is.

What's Actually True

Here's why the magic number falls apart the moment you look closely at it.

Two people can retire with exactly the same amount of money — say, $1,000,000 — and end up in completely different situations.

One of them has a paid-off house, a pension, and modest tastes. The other has a mortgage, no pension, and a lifestyle that costs twice as much every month.

One of them retires at 62, healthy, with a spouse who's still working. The other retires at 68 with medical bills already piling up.

Same number. Completely different reality.

That's because $1,000,000 isn't a plan. It's just a pile of money. What actually determines whether you'll be okay isn't the size of the pile — it's what you're asking that pile to do.

- How much income does it need to produce every month?
- How long does it need to last?

- What else is helping to support you — Social Security, a pension, part-time work?
- How much of your spending is essential, and how much is flexible?
- What happens if the market has a bad year right when you need to start withdrawing?

None of those questions are answered by a specific number. They have to do with the relationship between what you have and how you plan to use it.

That's the shift this book is going to walk you through. Not "how much do I need," but "what does my plan actually need to do — and does it do it?"

That second question is harder to put on a bumper sticker. But it's the one that actually tells you whether you're going to be okay.

The number was never the answer.

Practical Takeaway

Stop asking, "Do I have enough money?"

Start asking, "Does my plan cover my life?"

Your number might be $400,000. It might be $2.5 million. On its own, that number tells you almost nothing. What matters is whether it lines up with your spending, your income sources, your health, and the life you actually want to live.

Two people. Same number. Different outcomes. That's not an exception — that's the rule. And once you understand why, you stop measuring your retirement against a headline and start measuring it against your own life, which is the only comparison that ever mattered.

Action Step

Before you read any further, do this one simple exercise.

Grab a piece of paper — or open a blank note on your phone — and write down two lists.

List 1: Guaranteed income. Anything that shows up every month no matter what the market does — Social Security, a pension, an annuity.

List 2: Monthly expenses you can't avoid. Housing, food, insurance, medications — the things you'd pay even in a bad year.

Now compare them.

If List 1 covers most of List 2, you're closer to "okay" than that scary number ever told you. If there's a big gap, that gap — not some faraway magic number — is the real thing you need a plan for.

Don't worry if the gap surprises you. Clarity is progress.

This is the first step in trading a guess for an answer.

YOUR MONTHLY GAP

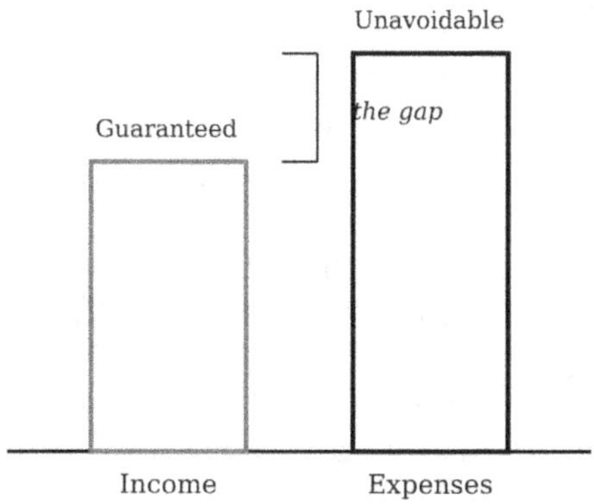

The gap between them
is what actually needs a plan.

- The idea that a single savings number determines whether you'll be okay is a myth.
- Two people with identical savings can have very different retirement outcomes.
- What matters isn't how much you have — it's whether your plan matches your income, spending, health, and lifestyle.
- The right question isn't "How much do I need?" It's "Does my plan cover my life?"
- Your first step: compare your guaranteed income to your unavoidable expenses. The gap between them is what actually needs a plan.

Retirement doesn't begin the day you stop working. It begins the day you stop wondering if you're going to be okay.

Chapter 2: Why Most Retirement Calculators Ask the Wrong Question

Meet Linda

Linda found the calculator on a Tuesday night.

She'd been putting it off for months — that nagging feeling that she should "run the numbers" before she gave notice at work. So she sat down at the kitchen table, opened her laptop, and typed her age, her savings, and her expected retirement date into a free online calculator.

She hit "Calculate."

A single word appeared on the screen, in bold, friendly green letters:

"On Track!"

Linda felt a wave of relief. She closed the laptop, poured a cup of tea, and told herself she could finally stop worrying.

For the first time in months, she slept well.

Three weeks later, her sister asked her a simple question over the phone: "What happens if you need long-term care at some point? Did the calculator ask about that?"

Linda paused.

It hadn't.

It hadn't asked about her mother's history of memory issues. It hadn't asked whether she planned to help her adult son with a down payment. It hadn't asked what she'd do if the market dropped 30% the year she retired. It had just taken a few numbers, run them through a formula, and handed her two comforting words.

"On Track" started to feel less like an answer and more like a guess wearing a lab coat.

What People Believe

Most people believe a retirement calculator can tell them if they're going to be okay.

Type in some numbers, get a green checkmark, and you're set. It feels objective. It feels scientific. It feels like the internet did the hard work so you don't have to.

What's Actually True

Here's what most retirement calculators actually do: they take a handful of assumptions — your current savings, an average market return, a life expectancy, maybe an inflation rate — and run them through a formula.

That's it. That's the whole trick.

The calculator wasn't wrong. It just answered a much smaller question than Linda thought she was asking.

The problem isn't that calculators are useless. The problem is that they're only as good as the questions they ask — and most of them ask far too few.

A typical calculator might ask:

- How much have you saved?
- When do you want to retire?
- What return do you expect?

But real life asks harder questions than that:

- What happens if you need assisted living for five years?
- What if your spouse passes away and your household income drops, but your expenses don't?
- What if you retire right before a market downturn, and you're forced to sell investments at a loss just to pay your bills?
- What if inflation runs hotter than the calculator assumed?
- What if you want to help a grandchild with college, or a child going through a hard time?

A calculator built on averages can't see your life.

It doesn't know your marriage.

Your health.

Your family.

Or the life you're trying to build.

It only knows numbers.

It doesn't know about your mother's diagnosis, your son's student loans, or the fact that you've always dreamed of traveling for the first five years of retirement and slowing down after that.

That's not a flaw. It's a limitation. It's built into what a calculator is — a tool that measures numbers, not a tool that understands a life.

This doesn't mean calculators are worthless. They're a fine starting point. The danger isn't using a calculator. It's stopping there.

The mistake is treating the output as an answer instead of what it really is: a rough sketch that leaves out almost everything that makes your retirement yours.

A calculator can measure your money. It can't measure your life.

Practical Takeaway

A calculator can tell you whether your numbers line up with a formula.

It can't tell you whether your plan will survive contact with your actual life.

Think of a calculator result the way you'd think of a weather forecast. "70% chance of sun" is useful information. But you'd still bring an umbrella if you knew a storm hit your neighborhood every single year around this time, no matter what the forecast said. A calculator should inform your judgment — not replace it.

Action Step

Take the last calculator result you got — or run a free one if you haven't yet — and next to it, write down three things it didn't ask about.

Some places to start:

- A health condition that runs in your family
- Support you might want to give (or might need from) family members
- A big one-time expense you're planning — a wedding, a move, a home renovation
- How you'd feel, and what you'd actually do, if the market dropped sharply the year you retired

You don't need answers yet. You just need to see, in black and white, everything the green checkmark left out. That gap is where the real planning begins.

Retirement Reality Check

- A retirement calculator only sees the few inputs you give it — it doesn't see your life.

- "On Track" from a calculator is a starting point, not a verdict.
- Real retirement planning has to account for things calculators usually miss: health changes, family support, market timing, and one-time expenses.
- Use calculators for a rough estimate, not a final answer.
- Your first step: list what your last calculator result didn't ask about. That's where your real plan starts.

Chapter 3: The Questions People Really Want Answered

Meet Carol

Carol had a folder.

Not a fancy one — just a plain manila folder she kept in the drawer next to her bed. Inside were printouts from three different retirement calculators, two magazine articles, a napkin with numbers scribbled on it from a dinner conversation with her brother-in-law, and a sticky note that just said "ask CPA???"

She'd been collecting this folder for two years.

Every time she read an article or watched a video, she added something to it, hoping that eventually all the pieces would add up to an answer. But every time she opened the folder, she felt the same thing: more information, and somehow, less clarity.

One night her husband found her sitting on the bed, folder open, papers spread across the comforter.

"What are you looking for?" he asked.

Carol thought about it for a second.

"I just want someone to tell me the truth," she said. "Am I behind? Can I actually retire early like I want to? Will the money last? What happens if the market crashes the year after I quit?"

Her husband looked at the folder, then back at her.

"Have any of those articles actually answered your question?"

Carol laughed, a little sadly. "No. They just make me feel like I should already know."

What People Believe

Most people believe there's an expert somewhere with a simple, universal answer to their biggest retirement questions.

Somewhere out there, a financial guru, a calculator, or a bestselling book has the real answer to "Am I behind?" or "Will my money last?" — and if you just read enough, search enough, or ask enough people, you'll eventually find it.

What's Actually True

Here's the uncomfortable truth: those questions don't have universal answers. They only have personal ones.

"Am I behind?" Behind whom? Compared to what? Behind is a moving target that depends on your expenses, your health, your family, and what kind of retirement you actually want. A person who wants to travel the world every year is behind at a very different number than a person who wants to stay close to home and garden.

"Can I retire early?" That depends entirely on how much income your savings can safely produce, how long you need that income to last, and how flexible you're willing to be if things don't go as planned.

"Will my money last?" Nobody can answer that with certainty — not you, not a calculator, not even the most credentialed advisor in the country. What can be answered is a more useful question: how much risk is built into your plan, and what would have to go wrong for you to run into trouble?

"What if the market crashes?" This one actually does have a good answer, but it's not a number — it's a plan. A plan for which accounts you'd draw from first, how you'd adjust spending temporarily, and how much cash cushion you're keeping so you're never forced to sell investments at the worst possible time.

Notice the pattern. Every one of these questions feels like it wants a single number in response. Real retirement questions rarely have universal answers. They have personal ones. But every single one of them is actually a question about your specific situation, dressed up as a universal mystery.

That's exactly why Carol's folder couldn't help her. It was full of generic answers to a set of deeply personal questions.

The questions were never the problem. The answers were aimed in the wrong direction.

THE QUESTIONS EVERYONE ASKS

"Am I behind?"

"Can I retire early?"

"Will my money last?"

"What if the market crashes?"

Universal questions.
Personal answers.

Practical Takeaway

Stop searching for the article that finally has the answer. Start building the specific information that turns your questions into things that can actually be answered — your expenses, your income sources, your timeline, and your tolerance for risk.

The moment you make these questions personal instead of universal, they stop being unanswerable mysteries and start becoming a plan you can actually build.

Confidence begins the moment your retirement questions become personal instead of universal.

Action Step

Take the four big questions from this chapter and rewrite each one, replacing the vague version with a version specific to you.

Instead of "Am I behind?" try: "What do I need my savings to produce every month, and how close am I to that today?"

Instead of "Will my money last?" try: "What withdrawal rate would let my savings last 30 years, and am I currently under or over that?"

You don't need the answers yet. You just need better questions. That alone is progress most people never make.

Retirement Reality Check

- Big retirement questions like "Am I behind?" or "Will my money last?" feel universal, but the real answers are always personal.
- Generic articles and calculators can't answer personal questions — no matter how many you collect.
- "What if the market crashes?" is better answered with a plan than with a prediction.
- Turning vague questions into specific ones is the real first step toward clarity.
- Your first step: rewrite your biggest retirement question in terms of your own numbers, not a general rule of thumb.

Chapter 4: The Four Parts of Every Retirement Plan

Meet James

James liked to build things. Forty years as a contractor will do that to a person. He understood structure — foundations, framing, load-bearing walls. So when he started thinking seriously about retirement, he assumed it would work the same way.

"I just need the number," he told his financial advisor. "Give me the target, and I'll hit it."

His advisor, a patient woman named Patricia, smiled. "It's not really one number, James. It's more like four."

James frowned. "Four numbers?"

"Four parts," she said. "Think of it like one of your houses. You wouldn't judge a house by the size of the foundation alone. You'd look at the foundation, the framing, the roof, and how well it all holds together in a storm."

James smiled.

For the first time, retirement didn't feel like a number.

It felt like something he knew how to build.

"So what are the four parts?"

Patricia pulled out a blank sheet of paper. Across the top she wrote four words.

Income.

Spending.

Time.

Flexibility.

"This," she said, "is your retirement plan."

What People Believe

Most people believe their retirement plan is really just about one thing: how much they've saved.

Save enough, and everything else takes care of itself. It's the belief behind Robert's story in Chapter 1 — the idea that a single pile of money, by itself, is the whole plan.

What's Actually True

A retirement plan isn't one thing. It's four things, working together:

Income. This is everything coming in — Social Security, a pension, part-time work, rental income, and withdrawals from your savings. Income is what actually pays your bills. Savings on their own don't pay anything; income does.

Spending. This is what actually goes out the door every month. Not what you think you'll spend — what you actually spend, including the expenses that sneak up on you: home repairs, gifts, medical costs, and the occasional splurge that makes retirement worth having.

Time. This is how long your plan needs to work. Not just your life expectancy — but the possibility that you, or a spouse, live well beyond average. Time is the silent variable that turns a good plan into a great one, or a good plan into a risky one, depending on how it's handled.

Flexibility. This is your ability to adjust when life doesn't go according to plan — and it never fully does. Flexibility might mean delaying a big purchase in a bad market year, working part-time a little longer than planned, or having a cash cushion so you're never forced into a decision you didn't want to make.

A retirement plan isn't judged by its strongest pillar. It's judged by its weakest one.

Here's what James's advisor helped him see: a retirement plan is strong when all four parts support each other, and it's shaky when even one of them is ignored.

You can have plenty of income but no flexibility, and one bad year wrecks you. You can have modest spending but no cushion for time, and you outlive your plan. You can have a great savings number, but if your spending assumptions are wrong, the number was never the real story anyway.

This is why "How much should I save?" is the wrong first question. The right first question is: "How do these four parts fit together for my life?"

A retirement plan doesn't become stronger because one pillar gets bigger. It becomes stronger when all four work together. Your retirement isn't built on one pillar. It stands on four.

YOUR RETIREMENT PLAN

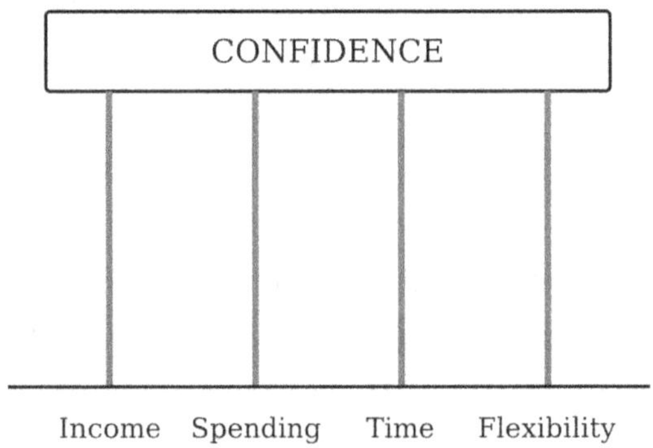

A retirement plan isn't judged by its strongest pillar.

It's judged by its weakest one.

Practical Takeaway

Before you obsess over your savings number, take stock of all four parts of your plan. A house with a strong foundation but a weak roof still leaks. Retirement works exactly the same way. A retirement plan with strong savings but no flexibility still breaks under pressure.

Action Step

Draw four boxes on a page — Income, Spending, Time, Flexibility. Under each one, write a single honest sentence describing where you currently stand.

You don't need it to be complete or perfect. You just need to see, clearly, which of the four pillars is strongest right now — and which one needs the most attention.

Now ask one more question: which pillar would make the biggest difference if it improved by just one point?

Retirement Reality Check

- A retirement plan isn't one number — it's four parts working together: Income, Spending, Time, and Flexibility.
- Strong savings alone can't compensate for weak flexibility or unrealistic spending assumptions.
- Time isn't just life expectancy — it's the risk of living longer than average, for you or a spouse.

- Flexibility is what lets a plan bend instead of break when life doesn't go as expected.
- Your first step: write one honest sentence under each of the four pillars to see where your plan is strong — and where it isn't.

Chapter 5: Why Two People With the Same Savings Have Different Outcomes

Meet Denise and Frank

Denise and Frank weren't married to each other. They'd never even met. But their financial advisor, coincidentally, worked with both of them — and both retired the exact same year, with the exact same amount saved: $1,000,000.

Denise retired at 63. Her house was paid off. She had a small pension from years as a schoolteacher, plus Social Security starting at 65. Her biggest indulgence was visiting her grandkids twice a year and keeping her garden stocked with more tomato plants than any one person needs.

Frank retired at 63 too. He still owed eleven years on his mortgage. He'd never had a pension. He was supporting an adult son who'd moved back home after a rough divorce, and he had a lifestyle built around two vacations a year, a boat he loved, and a habit of picking up the check at family dinners.

Five years later, Denise's plan was humming along quietly. Her advisor barely had to adjust anything.

Frank's plan was in trouble. He'd had to sell the boat, help his son find his own place sooner than he could really afford, and cut back on the vacations he'd promised himself for decades.

Same amount saved.

Same retirement year.

Same advisor.

Completely different retirements.

What People Believe

Most people believe that if two people save the same amount of money, they'll have roughly the same retirement.

The number does the talking. If Denise and Frank both have $1,000,000, the assumption is that they're both equally "ready" — equally safe, equally comfortable, equally set.

What's Actually True

The truth is that $1,000,000 never promised the same retirement. It was just a starting point — and what happened next depended on everything except the number itself.

Denise's paid-off house meant a huge chunk of her monthly expenses simply didn't exist. Frank's mortgage meant a big, fixed bill every single month, for years, no matter what the market did.

Denise's pension and Social Security together covered most of her basic needs. Frank had no pension at all, which meant his $1,000,000 had to work much harder, covering a bigger share of his monthly income.

Denise's spending was modest and mostly optional — tomato plants and plane tickets to see grandkids. Frank's spending included obligations that didn't feel optional in the moment: helping his son, keeping promises to his family, maintaining a lifestyle he'd built over decades.

None of this makes Frank a bad planner or Denise a lucky one. It simply shows that the number was never the whole story. The real story was in the four pillars from the last chapter — Income, Spending, Time, and Flexibility — and how differently they showed up in two lives that, on paper, looked identical.

This is why comparing your retirement to a friend's, a neighbor's, or a headline's "average" savings figure is almost always misleading. You're not just comparing bank balances.

You're comparing two entirely different lives...

wearing the same number as a disguise.

The same number can tell two completely different stories. Money tells you how much people have. It rarely tells you how they live.

Practical Takeaway

Stop comparing your savings to anyone else's — a coworker's, a sibling's, or a statistic from an article. The number by itself tells you almost nothing about whether someone is actually going to be okay. What matters is how that number interacts with their specific mortgage, income sources, family obligations, and lifestyle.

Your job isn't to match someone else's number. It's to understand how your own number performs against your own life.

Action Step

Think of one person whose retirement savings you've compared yourself to — even quietly, even just once.

Now write down three ways your situation is actually different from theirs: your housing costs, your income sources, your family obligations, your health, anything that changes the equation.

This isn't about judging their choices or yours. It's about breaking the habit of measuring your retirement against a number that was never built to describe your life in the first place.

Retirement Reality Check

- Two people with identical savings can have completely different retirement outcomes.

- Housing costs, pensions, family obligations, and lifestyle all shape how far a savings number actually goes.
- Comparing your savings to someone else's is comparing two different lives wearing the same number.
- The four pillars — Income, Spending, Time, Flexibility — explain the gap that the raw number never shows.
- Your first step: pick one comparison you've made in your head and write down what actually makes your situation different.

Chapter 6: The Hidden Retirement Risks

Meet Margaret

Margaret had done everything right, or so she thought.

She'd saved diligently for thirty years. She'd paid off her house. She'd run the numbers through three different calculators, and every single one had told her the same reassuring thing: she was ready.

What none of them warned her about arrived quietly. It showed up one at a time, like uninvited guests arriving at a party she thought was already over.

The first year, her property taxes and healthcare premiums rose faster than she'd budgeted for. Her grocery bill, which she'd assumed would stay flat, crept up year after year until it was nearly 40% higher than when she'd retired.

The second year, the market dropped sharply, right as she needed to start taking withdrawals. She watched her account balance fall just as she was pulling money out of it — a double blow she hadn't fully understood was possible.

The third year, her sister was diagnosed with a condition that ran in their family. Margaret quietly began wondering, for the first time, how long she herself might live — and whether her plan had ever really accounted for that.

None of these things were disasters on their own. But together, they were the risks nobody had warned her about clearly enough, back when she still had time to plan for them.

What People Believe

Most people believe the biggest retirement risk is simply running out of money because they didn't save enough.

Save more, the thinking goes, and you eliminate the risk. It's a comforting idea, because it makes the solution simple: work harder, save harder, and you'll be safe.

What's Actually True

Under-saving is a real risk. But it's far from the only one — and often, it's not even the most dangerous one.

Inflation quietly raises your cost of living every year, even when nothing dramatic happens. It doesn't announce itself. It simply asks your money to do more every year. A grocery bill that feels manageable today can become a real strain a decade from now, especially if your income doesn't rise to match it.

THE QUIET CLIMB

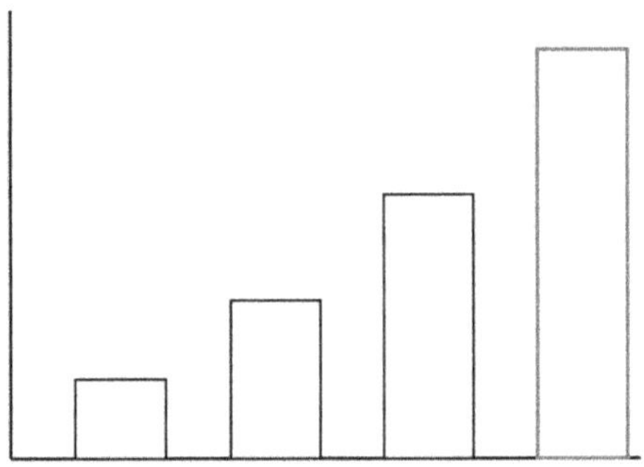

Same grocery list. Quietly larger bill, every year.

It doesn't announce itself.
It just asks your money to do more.

Taxes don't disappear in retirement. They simply change shape. Withdrawals from certain accounts are taxable income. Required withdrawals at a certain age can push you into a higher bracket than you expected. A plan that ignores taxes isn't really a full plan.

Healthcare costs tend to rise faster than everyday inflation, and they tend to rise fastest exactly when you're least able to absorb a shock — later in retirement, when income is more fixed and expenses are less flexible. Few retirees expect healthcare to become one of their largest expenses. Many discover it after they've already retired.

Sequence of returns is the risk Margaret felt firsthand: the order in which market gains and losses happen matters enormously. A market drop in your first few retirement years can do far more damage than the same drop happening a decade later, because you're withdrawing money at the same time your investments are losing value.

Longevity is the risk of living longer than your plan assumed — which sounds like good news, until you realize it means your money has to last longer too. Many people plan around an "average" life expectancy, without considering that half of all people live longer than average, sometimes by twenty years or more. Outliving your money isn't caused by living too long. It's caused by planning for too short a life.

None of these risks make headlines the way "market crash" does. They're quieter, slower, and easier to ignore — right up until they aren't.

The risk that gets you... isn't usually the one you were watching for.

Retirement doesn't fail because one thing goes wrong. It struggles when several ordinary things happen at the same time.

THE HIDDEN RISKS

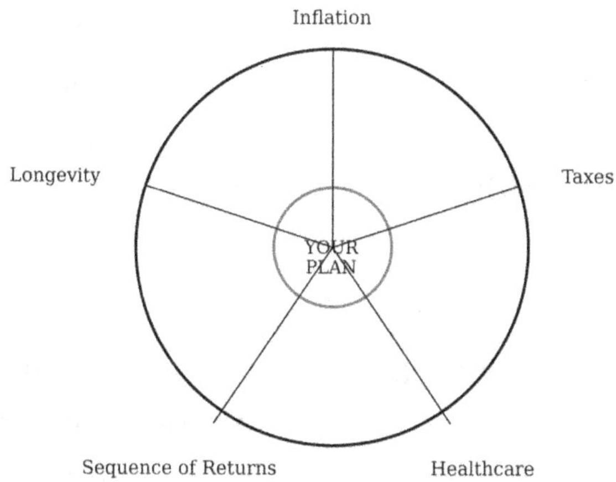

Five quiet risks.
One plan that has to hold them all.

Practical Takeaway

A retirement plan that only guards against running out of savings is only guarding against one risk out of five. Inflation, taxes, healthcare, sequence of returns, and longevity all deserve their own honest look — not because they're guaranteed to happen, but because ignoring them doesn't make them less likely.

Action Step

Go through the five hidden risks in this chapter — inflation, taxes, healthcare, sequence of returns, longevity — and next to each one, write a single sentence: has your plan actually accounted for this, or has it just assumed it away?

You don't need to solve all five today. You just need to know which ones are currently invisible in your plan, because those are the ones most likely to surprise you later.

Retirement Reality Check

- Running out of savings isn't the only real retirement risk — it's just the most obvious one.
- Inflation and healthcare costs tend to rise faster than people expect, especially later in retirement.
- Taxes don't disappear in retirement; they change shape and still need planning.

- Sequence of returns risk means the timing of market losses can matter more than the losses themselves.
- Longevity risk means planning for “average” life expectancy may leave half of all retirees underprepared.
- Your first step: check each of the five hidden risks against your own plan, one honest sentence at a time.

Chapter 7: Retirement Myths That Cost People Money

Meet Tom

Tom was proud of how much he knew about retirement.

He'd read the books. He'd watched the shows. He had opinions — strong ones — about withdrawal rates, Social Security timing, and market trends, and he shared them freely at every family barbecue.

So when he sat down with a retirement planner his daughter had recommended, he expected to hear that he was ahead of the game.

Instead, the planner gently took apart, one by one, almost everything Tom believed to be true.

"You said you're planning to claim Social Security at 62 because you're worried it'll run out. But have we looked at what waiting would actually mean for your monthly benefit?"

"You said you want to keep your investments conservative now that you're retired. But if you're retired for 30 years, is 'safe' really the same thing as 'safe long-term'?"

"You said your rule of thumb is to withdraw 4% no matter what. But is that rule built for someone retiring at 60, or someone retiring at 70?"

By the end of the conversation, Tom wasn't embarrassed.

He was relieved.

For the first time, someone had explained why the rules didn't always fit the people. For years, he'd been making decisions based on things he'd heard repeated so often, he'd never thought to question them.

What People Believe

Most people believe the popular rules of thumb they've heard repeated for years are simply true — because everyone says them.

If enough people repeat something at enough barbecues, on enough shows, in enough articles, it starts to feel like established fact, even when it was never actually tested against a specific situation.

What's Actually True

Some of the most common retirement advice is surprisingly expensive.

Myth: Claim Social Security as early as possible, just in case it runs out. For many people, waiting a few extra years significantly increases the monthly benefit for the rest of their life — sometimes by 60% to 80% compared to claiming at the earliest age. The right age to claim depends on health, other income, and household situation — not fear of a headline.

Myth: Get conservative with investments the moment you retire. A 65-year-old today may need their money to last 25 to 30 years. Being too conservative too early can mean running out of growth exactly when inflation and healthcare costs are working against you.

Myth: The 4% withdrawal rule works for everyone. That rule was built around a specific set of assumptions — a certain retirement length, a certain investment mix, a certain market history. Someone retiring at 55 has very different needs than someone retiring at 72. A rule of thumb is a starting conversation, not a finish line.

Myth: Paying off the house before retiring is always the smart move. For some people, yes. For others, keeping a low-rate mortgage and letting other investments grow can leave them better off. It depends entirely on the specific numbers — not a blanket rule.

Myth: You'll spend less in retirement, so you don't need as much as you think. Some expenses do drop. Others — healthcare, travel, helping family — often rise. Assuming a lower number across the board can leave a real gap.

None of these myths are stupid. They're simplified truths that got repeated so often, the nuance disappeared. And nuance, it turns out, is usually where the real money is.

A rule of thumb is a starting point. It was never meant to be your whole plan.

Rules are useful. Thinking is indispensable.

Practical Takeaway

The most expensive mistakes in retirement rarely come from ignorance — they come from confidently repeating something that sounded true, without checking whether it actually applied to your specific situation.

Action Step

Pick one retirement “rule” you’ve always believed — something you’ve heard so often you never questioned it. Write it down, then write one honest question next to it: does this actually apply to my age, my health, my income sources, and my goals — or did I just assume it did?

Retirement Reality Check

- Popular retirement rules of thumb aren’t necessarily wrong — but they’re rarely universal.
- Claiming Social Security early “just in case” can significantly reduce lifetime benefits for many people.

- Getting too conservative too early can leave a 25-to-30-year retirement short on growth.
- The 4% withdrawal rule was built on specific assumptions that don't fit every retiree.
- Paying off a mortgage isn't automatically the smartest move for everyone.
- Your first step: pick one belief you've never questioned, and ask whether it actually applies to you.

Chapter 8: Testing Your Retirement Plan

Meet Susan

Susan's son-in-law worked in software, and one day he said something that stuck with her.

"Before we launch anything," he told her, "we break it on purpose. We try to find every way it could fail before real people find those ways for us."

Susan had never thought about her retirement plan that way. She'd built it carefully — savings, an estimated budget, a rough withdrawal plan — but she'd never once tried to break it. She'd only ever looked at it on a good day, in a good year, assuming everything would go roughly as expected.

That week, almost as an experiment, she sat down and asked herself some uncomfortable questions. What if the market dropped 25% the year she retired? What if she needed a new roof and a new car in the same year? What if she lived to 98 instead of 85?

She didn't like every answer she found. But for the first time, she actually knew where her plan was strong — and where it would snap under pressure.

Oddly enough, she felt calmer than she had in months.

What People Believe

Most people believe "testing" a retirement plan means running it once through a calculator and checking that the ending balance stays positive.

If the number at the end doesn't go below zero, the plan must be solid. Test passed. Nothing more to check.

What's Actually True

A single, best-guess projection isn't really a test — it's a snapshot of one possible future, usually a fairly favorable one.

Real testing means deliberately trying to break your plan, the way Susan's son-in-law tried to break his software before real customers ever touched it.

Stress test for market timing. What happens if a serious downturn hits in your first few years of retirement, rather than smoothing out over decades the way average returns suggest? This is the sequence-of-returns risk from Chapter 6, made concrete.

WHY ORDER MATTERS

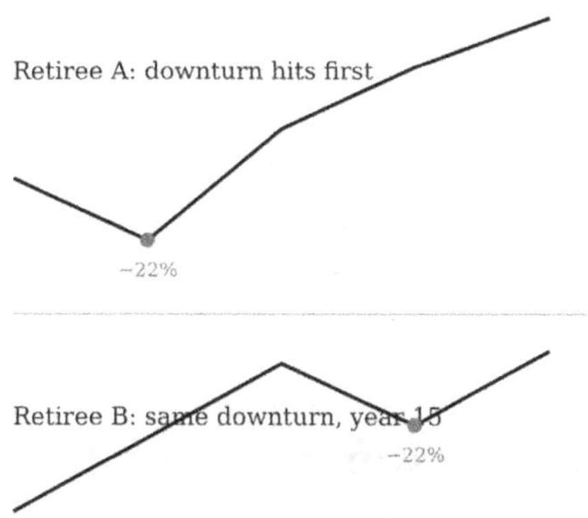

Same drop. Same size. Very different outcomes —
because withdrawals were already underway for Retiree A.

It's not just how much you lose.
It's when you lose it.

Stress test for spending shocks. What happens if two unplanned expenses hit in the same year — a health issue and a home repair, for instance? Real life rarely spaces out its surprises conveniently.

Stress test for longevity. What happens if you or your spouse lives well past average life expectancy? Does the plan bend, or does it break somewhere around year 25 or 30?

Stress test for inflation running hot. What happens if costs rise faster than expected for several years in a row, the way they did in the early 2020s?

Stress test for losing a spouse. What happens to household income and expenses if one spouse passes away — does Social Security or a pension drop in a way that leaves the survivor short?

None of these questions are meant to scare you. They're meant to show you, clearly, where your plan already handles pressure well, and where it needs reinforcement. A plan that survives every one of these stress tests isn't lucky. It's actually built to last.

Questions asked today become confidence tomorrow.

A plan that's never been tested is just a guess wearing a good outfit.

STRESS TEST YOUR PLAN

A plan that's never been tested
is just a guess wearing a good outfit.

Practical Takeaway

Don't judge your retirement plan by how it performs in a best-case scenario. Judge it by how it performs when things go wrong — because eventually, in some small way, they usually do.

Action Step

Pick just one stress test from this chapter — market timing, spending shocks, longevity, inflation, or losing a spouse — and walk through it honestly for your own situation. Where does the plan bend a little? Where does it actually break?

You don't need to test everything at once. You just need to start finding the cracks before life finds them for you.

Retirement Reality Check

- A single best-case projection isn't a real test of a retirement plan.
- Real testing means deliberately trying to break your plan under realistic pressure.
- Key stress tests include market timing, spending shocks, longevity, inflation, and the loss of a spouse.
- A plan that survives these tests isn't lucky — it's genuinely built to last.
- Your first step: pick one stress test and honestly walk your own plan through it.

Chapter 9: How to Stop Guessing

Meet Bill

Bill had spent thirty years as an engineer, and he liked to say that guessing wasn't part of his vocabulary.

But when it came to his own retirement, that's exactly what he'd been doing — for over a decade.

He guessed that his savings were probably enough, because a calculator once told him so. He guessed that Social Security would work out fine, because he hadn't looked closely at his own claiming strategy. He guessed that his spending would drop in retirement, because that's what he'd always heard. He guessed that the market would behave the way it always had, because it always had — until, of course, the one year it didn't.

None of these guesses were reckless. They were reasonable-sounding assumptions, repeated so often that they had started to feel like facts.

One day, sitting with a planner, Bill said something that surprised even him.

"I think I've been calling guesses a plan."

What People Believe

Most people believe that having a general sense of their finances — a rough savings number, a vague

plan, some optimism — is the same thing as having an actual retirement plan.

If it feels roughly fine, it must be roughly fine.

What's Actually True

By now, this book has walked through why that feeling of "roughly fine" is so often built on sand:

There's rarely a single magic number (Chapter 1). Calculators only measure what you tell them to measure (Chapter 2). The big questions — am I behind, will my money last — only have personal answers, not universal ones (Chapter 3). A real plan is four pillars working together, not one savings figure (Chapter 4). Two people with identical savings can end up in completely different places (Chapter 5). Hidden risks like inflation, taxes, healthcare, sequence of returns, and longevity rarely show up in a quick mental estimate (Chapter 6). Popular rules of thumb are often myths dressed up as facts (Chapter 7). And a plan that's never been stress-tested is really just an untested guess (Chapter 8).

Put all of that together, and the pattern becomes obvious: guessing isn't a small, occasional mistake. For most people, it's the default state — not because they're careless, but because nobody ever showed them a clear alternative.

The alternative isn't complicated, even if it takes real effort. It looks like this:

Replace vague savings numbers with a clear picture of monthly income versus monthly expenses. Replace a single calculator result with an honest look at what it did and didn't ask about. Replace generic questions with specific ones built around your actual life. Replace a single savings figure with an honest look at all four pillars. Replace comparisons to other people's numbers with an understanding of your own situation. Replace blind spots around inflation, taxes, healthcare, market timing, and longevity with a clear-eyed look at each one. Replace inherited rules of thumb with questions about whether they actually apply to you. Replace a plan that's never been tested with one that's been deliberately, honestly stress-tested.

None of this requires becoming a financial expert. It requires becoming an honest witness to your own life — willing to ask better questions than "does this feel okay?"

Retirement doesn't reward perfect people. It rewards honest planners.

Confidence isn't a feeling you talk yourself into. It's a plan you've actually checked.

FROM GUESSING TO KNOWING

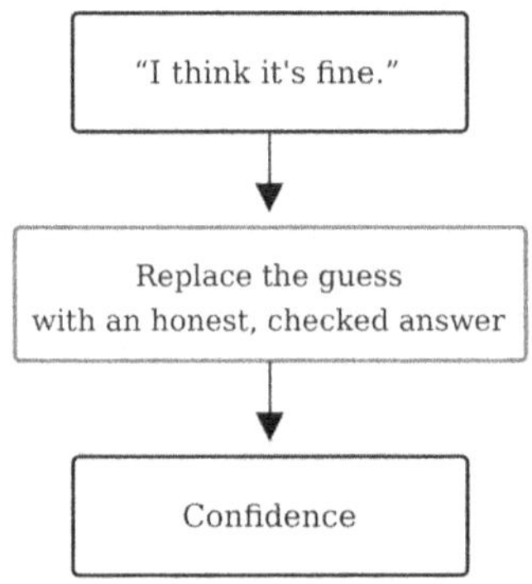

Confidence isn't a feeling you talk yourself into.

Practical Takeaway

The opposite of guessing isn't perfection. It's simply replacing assumptions with honest answers, one piece at a time, until your plan reflects your actual life instead of a rough feeling about it.

Action Step

Look back through the Action Steps in Chapters 1 through 8. Circle the one you haven't actually done yet — the exercise you read, nodded along to, and quietly skipped.

Do that one this week. Not all of them. Just that one. Progress toward confidence rarely comes from doing everything at once. It comes from finally doing the one thing you've been putting off.

Retirement Reality Check

- "Roughly fine" is a feeling, not a plan — and most people have been guessing without realizing it.
- Every myth this book has covered shares one thing in common: a vague assumption standing in for an honest answer.
- Replacing guesses with honest answers doesn't require financial expertise — it requires honest attention to your own life.
- Confidence comes from a plan you've actually checked, not a feeling you've talked yourself into.

- Your first step: go back and finally complete the one Action Step you've been putting off.

Chapter 10: Building Retirement Confidence

Meet Robert, Again

You remember Robert from the very first chapter — the man who hit $1,000,000, heard his wife say "You did it," and then lay awake that night, terrified that the number wasn't enough.

A year later, Robert is a different man. Not because his savings changed dramatically. Not because the market did him any special favors. He's different because he stopped guessing.

He sat down and mapped his guaranteed income against his real monthly expenses, the way Chapter 1 asked him to. He looked honestly at what his old calculator result had never asked about — his mother's health history, his son's occasional need for help, the vacations he actually wanted to take. He stopped comparing his number to his neighbor's number, once he understood, the way Denise and Frank taught us, that the same number can tell two very different stories. He checked his plan against inflation, taxes, healthcare, market timing, and longevity, instead of assuming those risks away. He questioned the rules of thumb he'd repeated for years without ever really testing them. And finally, he sat down and deliberately tried to break his own plan — a bad market year, a big surprise expense, a longer life than he expected — just to see where it held and where it didn't.

Robert still doesn't know exactly what the future holds. Nobody does. But he knows something he didn't know a year ago.

He knows what his plan can handle. And he knows what it can't — yet.

That distinction changed everything.

What People Believe

Most people believe that retirement confidence comes from reaching a certain number, a certain age, or a certain amount of good news.

Confidence, in this view, is something that arrives from the outside — a market that cooperates, a number that finally feels big enough, a headline that finally stops scaring you.

What's Actually True

Confidence was never going to come from outside. It comes from inside the work you've actually done.

Every chapter in this book pointed toward the same quiet truth: the number was never the answer, the calculator was never the whole picture, the questions were never as universal as they felt, the plan was never just one pillar, the comparisons were never fair, the risks were never as invisible as they seemed once you looked, the rules of thumb were never as solid as they sounded, and the plan was never tested until you tried, on purpose, to break it.

When you put it all together, a different kind of confidence emerges — not the loud, artificial confidence of hitting a magic number, but the quiet, durable confidence of knowing your plan has actually been built, checked, and stress-tested against real life.

This is the confidence Robert has now. Not certainty — nobody gets certainty. But clarity. He knows where his plan is strong. He knows where it's thin. And for the first time, "thin" doesn't scare him, because he knows exactly what to do about it.

That's the shift this entire book has been walking toward. Not from uncertainty to certainty — that's not realistic, and anyone who promises it isn't telling you the truth. But from guessing to knowing. From a vague hope that things will work out, to an honest, tested understanding of what your plan can handle and what it can't.

Retirement confidence isn't the absence of questions. It's finally having answered them.

THE CONFIDENCE JOURNEY

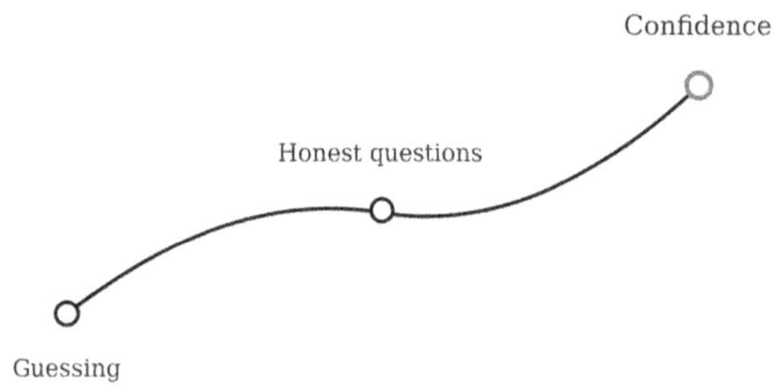

Retirement confidence isn't
the absence of questions.
It's finally having answered them.

Practical Takeaway

You don't need a bigger number to feel confident about retirement. You need a clearer answer. And a clearer answer comes from doing the honest, sometimes uncomfortable work this book has walked you through — not from waiting for a headline, a market, or a magic figure to finally make you feel safe.

Action Step

Go back to the very first page of this book, where you read about Robert lying awake, afraid, despite hitting his number.

Ask yourself the same question he asked that night: "Am I actually going to be okay?"

Now answer it — not with a feeling, but with everything you've built through this book: your income against your expenses, your four pillars, your honest look at risk, your tested plan.

That answer, built from real work instead of a guess, is the whole point of this book.

You won't control the market.

You won't control inflation.

You won't control how long you live.

But you can understand your plan.

And sometimes...

understanding is the closest thing we ever get to certainty.

Retirement Reality Check

- Real retirement confidence doesn't come from a bigger number — it comes from clarity you've built yourself.
- Every chapter in this book replaces a guess with an honest, checkable answer.
- The goal was never certainty. Nobody gets certainty. The goal was moving from guessing to knowing.
- A tested, honest plan turns "thin" spots into things you can act on, instead of things that scare you.
- Your first step: answer the question this book opened with — for yourself, using everything you've built.

Bonus Chapter: The Retirement Confidence Checklist

Everything in this book points toward one habit: checking your plan against reality instead of guessing.

That habit doesn't end when you finish this book. Retirement isn't a decision you make once — it's a plan you keep checking, year after year, as your life changes around it. This checklist is meant to be revisited annually, the way you'd check the oil in a car you intend to keep driving for thirty years.

Go through it once a year — maybe every January, or around your birthday. You don't need to score perfectly. You just need to know, honestly, where each item stands.

Income. Do you know exactly what's coming in every month — Social Security, pensions, part-time work, withdrawals — and whether it still matches what you assumed last year?

Spending. Has your actual spending drifted from your plan? Real life has a way of quietly raising the number every year.

Taxes. Have you reviewed how withdrawals, required distributions, and other income are affecting your tax bracket this year?

Inflation. Has your income kept pace with the rising cost of the life you're actually living, not just the one you budgeted for years ago?

Insurance. Are your health, long-term care, home, and life insurance coverages still appropriate for your current situation?

Estate documents. Is your will, trust, or power of attorney current — and does it reflect your life as it actually is today, not as it was when you first signed it?

Beneficiaries. Have you checked the beneficiary designations on your retirement accounts, life insurance, and annuities recently? These override your will, and they're easy to forget.

Healthcare. Have your healthcare costs changed, and does your plan still account for them realistically — including the possibility of needing more care than you do now?

Emergency fund. Do you still have a cash cushion set aside, so a surprise expense doesn't force you to sell investments at the worst possible time?

Stress test. Has it been a year since you last stress-tested your plan against a bad market, a big expense, or a longer life than expected? If so, it's time to run it again.

A plan you check once is a snapshot. A plan you check every year is a compass.

You don't need to overhaul your plan every January. You just need to look at it honestly, one item at a time, the same way you did the first time you read this book. That's not a one-time fix. That's what retirement confidence actually looks like, year after year.

Your Retirement Plan Checklist

YOUR RETIREMENT PLAN CHECKLIST

- [ ] Guaranteed income mapped
- [ ] Unavoidable expenses mapped
- [ ] Four pillars reviewed honestly
- [ ] Hidden risks checked, one by one
- [ ] Inherited rules of thumb questioned
- [ ] Plan deliberately stress-tested
- [ ] Big questions made personal

Retirement doesn't reward perfect people.
It rewards honest planners.

Take the Next Step

About the Author

Scott Grigsby is the founder of RetireWise AI, a company built around a single question: "Am I actually ready to retire?"

That question didn't start as a business idea. It started as a pattern he couldn't stop noticing — smart, disciplined people who had saved responsibly for decades, sitting across the table, still terrified they'd missed something. Not because they'd done anything wrong, but because nobody had ever shown them how to check their own work.

Scott built RetireWise AI to close that gap — combining retirement planning tools with plain-language guidance, so people could stop relying on a magic number they read in a headline and start understanding their own income, spending, risks, and plan clearly enough to trust it.

Retirement confidence matters to Scott because he's watched what its absence does to people. He's seen the sleepless nights, the frayed marriages over money nobody wanted to talk about, the early retirements delayed out of fear rather than necessity. He's also seen the other side of it — the relief on someone's face the moment their plan finally makes sense to them, not in theory, but in their own numbers.

He wrote this book because that relief shouldn't be limited to the people who happen to find their way into a consultation. The questions in this book are the same ones he's answered thousands of times in one-on-one conversations. He wanted them written down, in plain English, for anyone willing to sit with them honestly.

When he's not working on RetireWise AI, Scott spends his time doing what he hopes every reader of this book eventually gets to do without worry: living the life his own plan was built to support.

A Letter to the Reader

If you've read this far, thank you.

Not just for reading this book, but for staying with a conversation that isn't always easy.

Retirement has a way of bringing our biggest questions to the surface. Questions about money, certainly — but also about security, purpose, family, and whether we've done enough.

You didn't get a magic number in these pages. I hope by now you understand why.

What you gained instead is something sturdier: a way of looking at your own income, your own spending, your own risks, and your own plan clearly enough to answer one of life's biggest questions for yourself.

Am I actually going to be okay?

That's not as satisfying as a headline.

It's far more valuable.

Headlines disappear. Understanding stays with you.

So here's what I hope for you.

I hope you stop chasing numbers — the ones in magazines, the ones your coworkers repeat, the ones that were never meant to describe your life — and start trusting your own understanding instead.

If this book has helped you replace even a little uncertainty with understanding, then it has done exactly what I hoped it would do.

I wish you confidence in your decisions, peace in your retirement, and the freedom to spend less time worrying about your future — and more time living it.

And the next time someone asks if you're on track, I hope you don't reach for a guess.

I hope you reach for understanding.

Because that's where confidence begins.

Thank you for letting me be part of your journey.

Retirement doesn't begin the day you stop working.

It begins the day you stop wondering if you're going to be okay.

Scott Grigsby

Founder, RetireWise AI

www.ingramcontent.com/pod-product-compliance
Lightning Source LLC
LaVergne TN
LVHW022022200926
848481LV00007B/2496

* 9 7 9 8 9 9 6 9 8 2 4 0 0 *